CATS SET I

PERSIAN CATS

Tamara L. Britton
ABDO Publishing Company

visit us at
www.abdopublishing.com

Published by ABDO Publishing Company, 8000 West 78th Street, Edina, Minnesota 55439. Copyright © 2011 by Abdo Consulting Group, Inc. International copyrights reserved in all countries. No part of this book may be reproduced in any form without written permission from the publisher. The Checkerboard Library™ is a trademark and logo of ABDO Publishing Company.

Printed in the United States of America, North Mankato, Minnesota.
042010
092010

 PRINTED ON RECYCLED PAPER

Cover Photo: Photo by Helmi Flick
Interior Photos: Corbis pp. 8, 15, 21; Photo by Helmi Flick pp. 5, 7, 9, 10, 11, 12, 13, 17; Peter Arnold p. 19

Editor: BreAnn Rumsch
Art Direction & Cover Design: Neil Klinepier

Library of Congress Cataloging-in-Publication Data

Britton, Tamara L., 1963-
  Persian cats / Tamara L. Britton.
      p. cm. -- (Cats)
  Includes index.
  ISBN 978-1-61613-400-6
  1. Persian cat--Juvenile literature. I. Title.
  SF449.P4B75 2011
  636.8'3--dc22
                        2010014953

CONTENTS

LIONS, TIGERS, AND CATS

All **domestic** cats are descendants of African wildcats. More than 3,500 years ago, people in Egypt began taming these wildcats. The cats hunted rats and mice that threatened to eat stored grain.

Ancient Egyptians believed cats were sacred. Soon people in other countries began keeping cats, too. Eventually, these sociable creatures became companion animals.

Today, there are more than 40 different **breeds** of domestic cats. They belong to one of the 37 species in the family **Felidae**. Lions and tigers also are members of this family!

Persian cats

PERSIAN CATS

The Persian cat's exact beginnings are lost to history. Cat enthusiasts believe the Persian's ancestors are Angora cats from Turkey and long-haired cats from Persia, which is now Iran. These cats arrived in Europe in the 1600s.

In 1871, the first British cat show was held in London, England. Persian cats were among the 160 competitors.

Around this time, **breeders** in the United States began to import Persian cats. An 1895 cat show in New York City, New York, had 176 competitors. Some of them were Persians. The **Cat Fanciers' Association (CFA)** formed in 1906. The Persian was one of the group's original recognized breeds.

All long-haired cats are related to the Persian.

Over time, both British and American **breeders** mated Persians with the most desirable qualities. This careful breeding improved the Persian's special features. Eventually, the Persian developed into the fluffy, short-nosed cat we know today.

QUALITIES

Persians are gentle tempered and calm. They make sweet, loving pets. These affectionate cats enjoy a peaceful, secure home. Once they feel safe, they will be happy around children and other pets.

Persians don't like jumping or climbing. Some would even call these cats lazy! But Persians like to play and are very responsive to their owners.

Unlike **breeds** such as the Siamese, Persians are not very talkative. Instead, they communicate with their expressive eyes. Occasionally, they will use their quiet voice.

The calm, quiet Persian would be happy in an apartment.

Persians are famous for their large, round, beautiful eyes.

COAT AND COLOR

The Persian cat has a long, thick, flowing coat. This double coat has an outer layer of longer hairs

that guard a cottony undercoat. Thicker hair extends from the neck down the chest and between the front legs. Tufts of hair stick out from the ears and between the toes.

Persians come in many colors. The colors are divided into seven categories. They are solid, silver or golden, and shaded

Persians colored like Siamese cats are called Himalayans.

Calico coats are black, red, and white.

or smoke.
Other Persian colors
are tabby, **parti-colored**, calico
or **bicolored**, and Himalayan.
The Persian cat's eye color
depends on its coat color. It can
have blue, orange, gold, green, or
copper eyes. Some Persian cats
have eyes of two different colors!

SIZE

Persian cats are small to medium sized. Males range from 6 to 9 pounds (2.5 to 4 kg). Females range from 5 to 7 pounds (2 to 3 kg).

The Persian has a broad, round head and a short, thick neck. Its **muzzle** is short, and its nose is stubby.

The Persian's eyes are large and round. They are level rather

From the side, the Persian's nose does not extend past its forehead or chin!

than angled, and they are set far apart. The small ears are also set far apart. They are tilted slightly forward and end in rounded tips.

The Persian's short, stout body is well muscled. This sturdy cat has a broad chest and shoulders. Its short back leads to a rounded rear end that sports a bushy tail.

Short, thick legs support the Persian's robust body. Both front and rear legs are straight. They end in large, round paws.

CARE

Cats are naturally clean animals. They use their rough tongues to groom their coats. However, the Persian cat's abundant hair is hard for it to keep clean. A Persian's owner must have a strong commitment to its care and grooming.

A Persian's coat must be brushed thoroughly every single day. About every two weeks, the cat will need a bath after its daily brushing.

Tearstains will sometimes form under a Persian's eyes. While grooming your cat, wash its face to remove these stains. Daily washing will keep the stains from becoming permanent.

Cats instinctively bury their waste. So, a Persian can be trained to use a **litter box**. Keep the box in a quiet place away from the cat's food and water. Remove waste from the box daily.

Brushing your Persian's coat every day will prevent tangles. It will also keep hairballs from developing in the cat's stomach.

In the wild, cats sharpen their claws on trees. But because of its coat and grooming needs, a Persian should be kept indoors. So, it will need a scratching post where it can sharpen its claws.

Persians can develop medical problems, such as kidney trouble. It is important to develop a relationship with a veterinarian. He or she can provide your cat with yearly checkups and **vaccines**. The veterinarian can also **spay** or **neuter** the cat.

FEEDING

If you adopt a Persian cat, make sure it comes home with a bag of its food. Keep feeding your cat this familiar food. If you want to change brands, slowly mix in the new food with the old. This will prevent your cat from getting an upset stomach.

Cats are carnivores. They must eat food that contains meat. A cat also needs a balanced diet. Commercial cat food contains beef, poultry, or fish. There are three kinds of commercial cat food. They are dry, semimoist, and canned. Each will provide the **nutrients** a cat needs to be healthy.

The food's label will advise you on how much to feed your cat. The amount is based on the cat's age, weight, and health. Serve the food and plenty of fresh water in clean bowls.

Sometimes, your cat may enjoy a treat. But be careful with snacks between meals. Some indoor cats can become overweight. If you are concerned about your cat's weight, check with your veterinarian. He or she can recommend a proper feeding schedule.

Good food, fresh water, and frequent grooming will keep your Persian looking purrfect!

KITTENS

Female Persians are **pregnant** for about 63 to 65 days. The mother gives birth to about four kittens in each **litter**.

The kittens are born blind and deaf. They drink milk from their mother. When they are three weeks old, the kittens can see and hear. By then, they are playing and exploring. Their teeth are coming in, too. At this time, they begin to eat cat food.

Persian kittens should be gently cuddled every day. This will create calm, friendly pets. Early handling also prepares them for the daily grooming they need throughout their lives. When the kittens are 12 to 16 weeks old, they are ready to be adopted.

Though Persians are low-energy cats, they sometimes like to play. A sparkle ball or a catnip toy can provide hours of fun.

BUYING A KITTEN

If you have decided a Persian cat is the right cat for you, you are not alone. The Persian is the **CFA**'s number one cat! More Persian cats are registered with the CFA than any other **breed**.

You will need to decide if you want a show cat or a pet. The best place to get a show cat is from a breeder. Cat shows are also good places to find kittens.

The cost of a Persian depends on its **pedigree**. Kittens from award-winning parents can cost hundreds of dollars. You may also find Persian cats at shelters and rescue organizations.

When you decide on a kitten, check it closely for signs of good health. The ears, nose, mouth, and fur should be clean. Its eyes should be bright and clear. The kitten should be alert and interested in its surroundings. Your Persian cat will be a member of your family for 15 to 20 years.

With good care and lots of love, a Persian cat will be a loving companion many years.

GLOSSARY

bicolored - having two colors.

breed - a group of animals sharing the same ancestors and appearance. A breeder is a person who raises animals. Raising animals is often called breeding them.

Cat Fanciers' Association (CFA) - a group that sets the standards for judging all breeds of cats.

domestic - tame, especially relating to animals.

Felidae (FEHL-uh-dee) - the scientific Latin name for the cat family. Members of this family are called felids. They include domestic cats, lions, tigers, leopards, jaguars, cougars, wildcats, lynx, and cheetahs.

litter - all of the kittens born at one time to a mother cat.

litter box - a box filled with cat litter, which is similar to sand. Cats use litter boxes to bury their waste.

muzzle - an animal's nose and jaws.

neuter (NOO-tuhr) - to remove a male animal's reproductive organs.

nutrient - a substance found in food and used in the body. It promotes growth, maintenance, and repair.

parti-colored - having a dominant color broken up by patches of one or more other colors.

pedigree - a record of an animal's ancestors.

pregnant - having one or more babies growing within the body.

spay - to remove a female animal's reproductive organs.

vaccine (vak-SEEN) - a shot given to prevent illness or disease.

WEB SITES

To learn more about Persian cats, visit ABDO Publishing Company on the World Wide Web at **www.abdopublishing.com**. Web sites about Persian cats are featured on our Book Links page. These links are routinely monitored and updated to provide the most current information available.

INDEX